POST PANDEMIC WORKFORCE TRANSFORMATION.

~

The Future Of Work In The Post Pandemic Era

AMIT LOYD AUGUSTINE

COPYRIGHT

Table of Contents

INTRODUCTION

For years we having been discussing accelerated change. More than any other factor, the pace of transformation in business, economy, and society are through technological innovations has been remarkable. Remolding the eventual fate of work. However even as groundbreaking innovation has emerged over the years, the impacts of many of these innovations on how we get things done and

'work' is undeniable slow. That was the reality, up-on-till the global pandemic happened.

If the eventual fate of work is all about new working ethics, transformed roles of employees, maximizing potentials, fast learning, and reliability (due to limited physical supervision), as it is at the time of writing this book, then business are being forced to accept the reality that the future is here, as we face the global pandemic. As a technology advisor, consultant, and coach that advocates for enabling business growth through digital transformation, I have always talked about the importance of creating and implementing effective business solutions and strategies to get work done, as we face an unprecedented future. We are at long last and without a doubt, in dying need, such business solutions, and now is the time to reflect on every possible solution that makes the future workforce a reality in the present.

In the range of a couple of months, the world's economy has gone from a path of steady growth to facing massive cancellation of contracts, closure of businesses, and compulsory work from home measures. Top brand of the world cutting across all sectors are now struggling to virtualize business activities as social distancing keeps on being a must, to help "flatten the curve" of the infection. This global pandemic as it turns out might be the greatest catalyst for transformation in the way we do business and see the global workforce. As I have always predicted in my over one decade of career business technology world.

Where we once saw the future of work unfolding over years, we can all now see that with coronavirus as an accelerant, everything experts in the field have been predicting over the years, about the future of work is unfolding in a matter of months. With social distancing and sheltering in place, we're seeing changes that affect work, learning, and daily life, changes that will become a new normal and that take place against a backdrop of how the new workforce era will be a new normal post-pandemic. 'Offshore' was an old era, it's now called Remote working (Work from anywhere). Remote working is more economical, compared to traditional working style, saves cost, time, and energy, and makes employees more productive. The technology involved to support the entire shift will make all the difference.

Society as a whole has undergone radical changes as a result of the global pandemic. Among the most significant was the transition from in-office to remote work across various industries all over the world. The sudden surge in remote work created a cause for global discussion regarding best practices for bringing workforce teams together from afar. That is what this book is all about. To discuss and shield more light on what the future of work in a post-pandemic world will look like. This transformation is inevitable as I have always emphasized over the last decade. The question now on everyone's mind including business owners, employees, and customers is: How we are going to get the work done in a way that makes people feel safe, confident, productive, inspired, effective, and satisfied?

Join me as I take you on a journey through the Post Pandemic Workforce Transformation, highlighting everything you need to comprehend for you to remain relevant in the new reality of how we get work done. I will be throwing in my decade long experience in the business technology world and how businesses have strived even before, during, and after the pandemic with technology. This book takes us on a journey to the new reality, the new normal, which is our inevitable faith. I hope you find this book as insightful as expected and bring every strategy that applies to your business into the limelight. The future is now, so let's maximize the potentials of how we get work done in this new reality. With love, I, Amit Loyd Augustine welcome you to the new reality! You can reach out to me via LinkedIn https://www.linkedin.com/in/amit-loyd-augustine/

CHAPTER ONE

THE NEW WORKFORCE ERA AND IMPACT ON BUSINESS

More than half of the world's businesses and the workforce have been disrupted by the global pandemic that hit the world amidst uncertainties of what the future holds for us. Experts, professionals, and innovators saw these things coming, but the world decision-makers preferred to juxtapose and really on the realities at that time. Most businesses lack the resources to weather a months-long interruption, and forecasts indicate more than millions of workers tend to join the already spiked number of unemployed as a result of the coronavirus pandemic. There's likewise the possibility of new startups to experience a depression, where new organizations find it difficult to launch due to the elevated entry barriers as a result of the pandemic.

Likewise, amidst this global pandemic, businesses are adapting production capabilities to match the challenge of the new reality, as they implement measures to quickly respond to the necessary constraints of their workforces. The advisory that began as an abundance of caution quickly grew to a necessity as health officials recognized the greater risk of "community spread" of COVID-19: practice social distancing by working from home. Overnight, giant corporate campuses became ghost towns. Workers turned to Slack, Zoom, Skype, and Hangouts to meet, collaborate, and in many cases just to vent the understandable stress brought on by so much uncertainty. Still, in companies large and small, work goes on. Bosses are learning that out of sight does not mean out of mind. Workers are juggling deadlines and responsibilities even as family responsibilities become ever more present. Colleagues now need to talk, even more effectively. And with no other alternatives, managers are trusting their people to do the right thing.

Some companies will make the move to virtualization more seamlessly than others. Google and Microsoft, for example, have long relied on tools like Hangouts and Teams, respectively, to conduct business across offices and time zones. Others will struggle with policies that mandate where and how data can be processed, employee access to reliable high-speed bandwidth, and cultures that prioritize presence over productivity, among other obstacles.

Companies are finding it hard to adapt, and when this crisis recedes, I suspect many organizations will find that they can be highly efficient - and cost-effective - with distributed teams. They will alter policy and procedure to make remote work more available and in doing so recognize that they can tap a global pool of highly skilled workers. Layers of management will disappear along with very expensive physical plants, while investments in office space can be reallocated to salaries or other important things.

IMPACT OF THE GLOBAL PANDEMIC CUTTING ACROSS ALL SECTOR

Organizations must scale through the operational and financial complications from the global pandemic while swiftly tending to the necessities that will be helpful to survive this period. This chapter provides professional insights from a decade of experience combined with quantitative actions that can help your organization transform enormous unpredictability into significant change.

Effect on Strategies

How do businesses find the path to recovery and adopting new strategies? Organizations are confronted with overpowering, contending difficulties, and unknown waters as they keep on exploring the effects of the COVID-19 pandemic. Numerous businesses are as of now have taken strategic actions to rise out of the pandemic a better organization. These are the type of organizations confronting the global pandemic with a touch of reinventing and implementing quickened digital transformation, setting up variable cost strategies, and implementing agile operations for better performance in the post-pandemic world.

However, with the non-ending surge of the pandemic that continues to affect the majority of the business sectors and altering the return to normal activities of some others and amid this vulnerability, the process of reinvention and bouncing back to business as before. Yet, organizations have to take a critical observation of how this global pandemic in various topographies is affecting the strategies put in-place to possibly recuperate and go back to business.

Organizations must outsmart this vulnerability by amending their strategies, over and over again as the conditions surrounding the pandemic changes with every phase we encounter. Organizations are expected to reevaluate strategies, establish new expectations, and implement the right digital transformation tools to reinforce their capacity to detect trends and react effectively.

Effect on Customers

Organizations need to establish a new approach to connect with the transformed customer habits due to the pandemic. The global pandemic has caused organizations to begin to reexamine how to relate with customers, how employees convey vital customer experiences, and the channel through which products and services are offered, especially through digital means to help business coherence through this pandemic and in the post-pandemic world.

The global pandemic has drastically changed the expectations of customers from organizations which also reflects on how everybody's way of life has greatly changed over a short period. This new reality is practically changing how and what customers purchase and the impact of such change can be seen in the consumer products market, among many others. In the post-pandemic era, organizations need to consider the effect of these changes to customer behavior in transit to configuration, impart, develop and implement certain strategies to help meet up with the changing exceptions of the customers.

By developing and implement new practices, organizations have a chance to quicken their transformation to digital structures, by improving existing offers and establishing new offers, responding to customer demands by providing exceptional safer means of delivering products and services to customers. These transformations will cause businesses to rethink their way of doing business, implement strategies that bring about a new workforce era to be able to satisfy the catch new digital marketplace, and transformed customers.

Effect on Workforce

Businesses are encountering drastic workforce disruption on a global scale. For all intents and purposes, all organizations are as yet deciding how to function in the short term and eventually longer term, as the workforce and networks attempt to still work things done while battling to adapt to what's going on in their everyday lives due to the global pandemic.

As a business solution expert, I understand that Implementing innovative strategies across ventures is one key factor that is helping many organizations adapt to the situation, while helping individuals and associations explore gigantic workforce shifts, for example, the pressing need to move to a remote workforce for the protection and productivity of workers, in the way they offer service to clients and to set up business coherence. For instance, the now basic requirement for virtual consideration informing and visits in medicinal services.

There is a need for expertise in creating new dexterous workforce strategies to help keep organization in business as well as to keep the worldwide economy feasible and helping individuals and their families endure monetarily now and later on. Through digital innovations, organizations and businesses are now implementing new strategies to workforce active.

There is an urgent need to streamline the workforce to meet the changing work terrain by designing strategies that solve the immediate challenges while looking forward to improving on those strategies things continue to changes. Organizations, governments, and individuals all have a responsibility to carry out in setting up a new approach to boost workforce productivity with a safety-focused, digital-minded approach that advances shared workforce flexibility.

Effect on Operations:

With the global pandemic, major changes in buyers' behavior, supply chains, and means to make sales are kicking organizations out of business, there is a need to develop operational flexibility before any organization can strive. Reacting to the pandemic has underscored the requirement for business owners to quicken the implementation of digital solutions in operations and business networks to help overcome vulnerability in business.

The need to become a Digital Enterprise implies moving from top-down dynamic, engaging workforce guided by your need per time, driven by information, fueled by innovation, and empowered by cloud for effective and productive operations. There is a need to remove inflexible structures and establish a flexible operational module that fitting and purpose-driven. There is a need for digital transformation that brings about dynamic self-management of resources and continuous flexibility and adaptation of how we get work done. A new operational strategy that is developed for flexibility, agility, and development.

Implementing a shared universal operational model can likewise help businesses across various sectors to diffuse operational challenges. Automated routine strategies combining human, AI, and machine configurations, where every worker performs critical roles, will help improve how organizations will operation now, and for development in the post-pandemic era.

Also, presently, like never before, the need for the digital supply chain is paramount. Organizations need to create fast reactions to deliver current solutions and to reestablish and evolve the supply chains for the future by improving on the flexibility, adaptability, and obligation of their operations.

Effect on Finance

Building the assets to take advantage of new opportunities is important in the post-pandemic era. With the global pandemic, organizations have needed to act rapidly to streamline their organization's flexibility—restructuring for the worst and liquidity, while evaluating open doors for development in the post-pandemic era. Their survival relies upon quick transforming activity, including digital financial solutions for steadiness and vital flow of revenue that will develop new fates for organizations and sectors across the board.

These digital solutions are expected to address momentary liquidity challenges, yet additionally to resolve expenses and profitability issues while generating finances to put resources into a new use. Numerous organizations are confronted with falling deals and income and expanded expenses. The way out will involve investments in key innovations, models like EaaS, RPA; and knowledgeable individuals. For some organizations, liquidity is now the way out.

The deliberate actions taken by organizations now will determine their success in the long run, and how fast they can bounce back from the global downturn, and improve finances and ability to weather the storm in the future.

Effect on Technology

There is a need to build innovation for solidarity to succeed. Indeed, even before the emergence of the global pandemic, numerous organizations were confronted by extensive IT challenges. Due to the global pandemic, organizations are now pushed to quickly transform the way they work and technology is at the forefront facing the challenges squarely.

As organizations shuffle a scope of new frameworks needs and challenges, organizations continue to face challenges in coherence dangers, abrupt changes in work volume, the constant need to make decisions, workforce profitability, security risks, and organizations must act rapidly to address the reliability of their conventional framework and establish a new framework for what's to come.

If we arrive at the end of this pandemic, it will be imperative to set up long term procedures for more noteworthy adaptability and to apply knowledge gained from the experience to make frameworks and technological solutions that keep organization prepared for other disruptions in the future.

Effect on Industries

We need to transform all of these enormous challenges brought about by the global pandemic into significant change. Almost all sectors of the world are affected by the global pandemic, with changing degrees of seriousness. Some have more grounded resistances, while others will battle to come back to a continually changing normal known as the 'new normal.'

There is a change in customer behavior that reflects on the disruption of demand and supply, and different sectors, markets, and nations are reacting differently and remarkably to the global pandemic. Organizations will ceaselessly adjust to new and volatile economic conditions. With great insight from my over decade long experience in providing digital solutions to business across the world, further in this book, I offer industry-explicit tailored guidance on what organizations ought to consider doing now and in the post-pandemic era for a brighter future of the work.

REMOTE WORKING ~ THE NEW NORMAL

As organizations quickly adjust to the eventual fate of work at a quickened pace driven by the worldwide pandemic I see them grasping for innovative solutions for an empowering future. With attention to implementing the right strategies and tools, organizations can agilely transform business operations to flexible remote working while at the same time extending their ability through fast figuring out how to optimize operation lines and procedures to fulfill the changing needs of our present reality. Organizations no longer have the ability to keep workers under a roof as safety becomes the main challenges brought about by this worldwide pandemic.

Furthermore, for the first time in my career, I have seen the need to support people, human strength, and human creativity as vital. This is reflected in private ventures that despite their monetary losses are closing up their shops to ensure the safety of customers and staff while bigger organizations are losing revenue and gathering their extensive assets to support their immediate community and most vulnerable in the world at large. These are unnerving times, no doubt, and despite everything still have such a great amount to figure out. However, it is likewise an amazing hopeful period for the eventual fate of work for people. The business solutions and digital innovations we are implementing currently are confident signs that we humans will have an important role to work and livelihood transforms. There is a lot of vulnerability ahead and there is just a single route through this; which is through collaborations.

The front cover of a Time magazine in 2009 had an interesting highlight that stated "The Future of Work." and it went ahead to also state that "Discard your briefcases; you're not going to the workplace'" This statement when made back then caused a lot of disturbing controversies and lead to discussions around the eventual fate of work. Ever since the future of work has been a critical point of discussion, and everyone had to tag along in the long run.

For more than a decade, all we have been doing is to predict and imagine what this future may resemble. Now, the future is here, apparently suddenly, and has disrupted the whole of our reality. This global pandemic has overwhelmed the entire world by surprise and has also disrupted the global economy without the smallest notice. It has disrupted how we work and do business. Organizations are being prompted to implement lasting work-from-home strategies, and those that have been delaying implementation of digital transformation in their businesses are now abruptly on the verge of being obsolete.

In the unfurling COVID-19 pandemic, different frameworks and strategies are being tested more than ever. IT and business pioneers want their businesses to keep on working through this extraordinary disturbance by rapidly tending to the dependability of their basic business strategies and fundamental frameworks. The dependability of a framework portrays its capacity to work during a significant disruption or pandemic like this, with a negligible effect on basic business and operational procedures. This implies preventing business closure, moderating the impact of the disruption, or recuperating from them. Frameworks discussed in this book include applications like RPA, infrastructures, and networks like EaaS, data, information, cloud, and so on.

CHAPTER TWO

EMPLOYEE AS A SERVICE (EaaS) AND THE FUTURE OF WORK

The demand of the skilled workforce on a global base has birthed the reality for organizations to compete globally, increase flexibility and creativity. We cannot over emphasis the effect of the global pandemic and demographical changes on society and the workforce. It is crucial that policies that help organizations and business owners are implemented to manage the transition with the least possible disruption while maximizing the potential benefits are formulated.

The ability of businesses to attract rich but diversified intellectual mercenaries will be fundamental for the future of work, as flexible arrangements will become increasingly common with a workforce that consists, different groups of full-time employees (working remotely), contract, freelance talents, and others having no connection to a brand. I have seen the growth of on-demand services which range from Software as a Service (SaaS) to Infrastructure as a Service (IaaS) and now the need for Employee-as-a-service (EaaS).

"EaaS means renting employees/resources as per the requirements of the project on an as-needed basis, thus, allowing an organization to upscale or downscale their skill-set based on the project or work at hand." Organizations globally are experiencing workforce disruption at an unprecedented scale and speed. This is propelling EaaS into the spotlight of this human crisis.

EaaS has been and will continue to be a disruptive force in the labor market and the world without it is almost impossible to envisage today. Skill demands are changing so rapidly that even when a company lays out what it requires now, by the end of 2020 that will be different. From adaptability to building a brand, these are essential skills that workers will need to navigate a changing work environment and flourish in the next decade.

EAAS VS REMOTE WORKING

Remote workers are mostly engaged on full-time bases and overall cost remains the same or even high while paying even down-time and non-working hours. With EaaS, you can hire employees for one demand for specific hours on a daily, weekly, or monthly bases. This means that one employee can work for two clients if their work is less and this EaaS service is provided by selected technology vendors that would mean, the company can save more money and need not hire a full-time employee if work is only half of the actual time. Let us consider some benefits of EaaS in detail as we proceed.

IMPORTANCE OF EAAS

Ability to Focus More on Your Main Business Process

This is the most significant importance to EaaS in executing a basic business process. It's more effective to invest your energy doing whatever you're good at. In case you're a marketing organization, you ought to showcase products and services to your customers. What if you're a professional coach, you ought to mentoring some people. If you sell digital items, you ought to be working on making them.

In any case, there are a lot of errands on your plate that don't play to your skill. Possibly you aren't truly adept at dealing with your finances, performing client support, or rounding out HR services. Consistently taking a shot at undertakings outside of your range of abilities is time spent wastefully.

Most business people have extraordinary gifts, yet commonly they want to do everything. That can truly slow down the development of the business. By re-appropriating your work process to an expert on pay-as-you-need bases through EaaS providers you can have more opportunity to concentrate on other credible things.

It's quite often more financially savvy to use EaaS except for your main business offers. You'll set aside cash, maintain a strategic distance from pressure, and burn through your effort dealing with things you appreciate. It's quite often more cost-effective to use EaaS.

Reduction In Overhead and Labor Costs

Recruiting and preparing staff is costly, particularly for short tasks, and temporary engagement of skilled persons through EaaS most times produce the great work you need. At the point when you outsource, you convert fixed work costs into variable costs, which means you just pay for the services that you required. This gives you setting up adaptability that simply doesn't exist with in-house workers and better than have employees work remotely.

EaaS permits you to tailor your business consumption to your requirements. You just pay for what you utilize and can consistently scale your utilization when business improves or decrease. For example, you likely needn't bother with a full-time in-house auditor. However, it's a significant role that can't be disregarded, yet you don't have the resource to keep employees on full-time bases.

If you find one that will help you find talented experts who are happy to work only a couple of hours and get paid as they work. If you hire a full-time bookkeeper, for instance, they're probably going to leave you once they locate a better opportunity and there's no assurance they can work more when you have occasional necessities, such as during high demand hours.

With EaaS your bookkeeping services will be done by experts and you just pay for the administration you required yet hold the unwavering quality of a committed representative. Moreover, it's keen to exploit the workforce from a wide range of service providers even on an international base, however, recruiting individuals in different nations is an issue. At the point when you work with EaaS, they can deal with the aspect of providing a service provider with minimal pay, so you get top-notch services at a lower value point.

In-house staff or remote workers ordinarily come with their costs, as well, similar to office space, furniture, copier paper, and so on. Indeed, even the remote team comes with similar costs, such as hardware, access to programming devices, and connecting devices. These costs might not look big, but they increase your overall cost.

You might have the option to bring employee additional workers during the expansions process and if employing a new staff might mean moving to a larger and more expensive space, it might be less expensive to recruit via EaaS to address your issues. Then EaaS incorporates their expenses with the charges they charge, yet those overhead expenses are spread out over the entirety of several clients.

If the workers in your organization who uphold your main business process in your organization can cork from home, it may be conceivable to wipe out the greater part of your overhead expenses by re-appropriating all non-critical roles and transform your team to a work-from-anywhere course of action. This could make gigantic saving funds.

Control Cash Flow

At the point when you make use of EaaS, you convert a fixed cost (a full-time compensation) into a variable cost (a compensation for what-you-need). This opens up your more revenue for upholding other aspects of your business.

You could channel that money into improving your products and services, or running ad programs. This is particularly helpful at the beginning phases of new ventures, such as launching another product or venturing into another aspect of your business.

When you have any those that invested or you are planning to bring some, later on, they'll be satisfied to see loads of space in your revenue to put resources into income-producing exercises. An organization that isn't outfitted by lumbering fixed costs rushes to adjust to new thoughts or economic situations.

Moreover, re-appropriating services free you from putting resources into innovation or custom framework. For example, by working with an EaaS photograph producer, you wouldn't have to buy your photography gear or video altering programming. Those are things that the EaaS service provider will have. The ability to reduce the cost of production makes it a lot simpler for a company to strive during this global pandemic period.

Access to New Resources

Employing other staff frequently requires costly enlisting and training. You need to show them your procedures and work processes (or create unique procedures only for them). You may need to put resources into their training, so they have the correct abilities for your business. At the point when you make use of EaaS for your business requirements, the EaaS organization are the once to make sure service providers are knowledgeable about their offer

EaaS provides access to information, skill, and experience you might not be able to get from to recruit all alone. The EaaS is liable for any licenses or accreditation that the work requires. By concentrating on their claim to fame, re-appropriates remain side by side of industry changes and patterns, learn new strategies, and continually build up their abilities.

Besides, EaaS approach abilities and instruments you may not require today yet will sometime in the not so distant future. On the off chance that they don't have somebody on staff who can take care of your concern, they likely have a system of experts with corresponding aptitudes they can pull from. You don't have such adaptability with in-house representatives.

For instance, suppose you have a creator in your group, yet he has practical experience in print materials. He'll prepare an incredible pamphlet, yet he doesn't think a lot about computerized items.

At the point when it comes time for another site, your originator won't be a lot of help. On the off chance that you redistribute your plan work to an imaginative office, in any case, you will approach planners with a wide scope of abilities.

Controlling Risk

Worker turnover can be agonizing. At the point when somebody stops, all that cash you spent on employing and training follows the person through the entryway with them. Some turnovers come at the worse time (and is there ever a perfect time?) and can upset your tasks, causing exorbitant issues.

EaaS fabricates a degree of consistency in your business. If your HR leaves the organization at a crucial time, you would need to scramble to fill the position (perhaps employing the main adequate candidate, regardless of whether they weren't extraordinary), accomplish the work yourself, or just do without.

Yet, if you use EaaS for your work processes, your tasks would proceed easily without interference or hazard. You could depend on the assignments to be completed and the expenses to stay reasonable.

CHAPTER THREE

INTERNET OF THINGS AND THE POST PANDEMIC WORK FORCE

IoT is playing an important role in this transition to the post-pandemic workforce era, in several industries across boards. Teams in sectors such as manufacturing, healthcare, and supply chain can leverage IoT technologies to facilitate remote work. And as workforces enter the "new normal" that lies ahead, IoT devices in smart cities and homes can help them make this shift as smooth as possible too. Let's dive deep into how IoT is facilitating remote work now and will continue to power the "new normal" post-crisis.

IoT is playing a vital role in this transition period in several industries. The workforce in industries like production, medical care, and supply chain are taking advantage of IoT to promote working from home. As workforces across all sectors are experiencing the "new normal", IoT gadgets in tech-inclined urban cities and homes are helping them with making this transition seamless. How about we take a look at how IoT is presently driving remote work and how it will keep on contributing to the post-pandemic workforce era.

In these troublesome times, innovation has demonstrated to be one of the most remarkable partners any business can have. What's more, right now is an ideal opportunity to capitalize on it. Today I need to focus some light on how the internet of things (IoT) can enable any organization to strive through the pandemic.

HOW IOT POWERS REMOTE WORK

In the manufacturing sector, IoT allows employees to now carry out their responsibilities from different places. At this point when workers can't be present because of health issues and it becomes more suitable to work from home, they can keep tasks running easily due to innovative IoT management solutions.

These solutions are developed with IoT sensors and gadgets that can show when machines will require part maintenance or a complete overall, allowing workers to carry out such tasks remotely and remain productive with their functions. Rather than having people to perform assessments of machines, Industrial IoT sensors are conveying information as it happens about the conditions and recognize vibrations that exhibit a potential breakdown of equipment.

In the health care sector, businesses are making use of IoT-empowered remote patient observing innovation (RPM) to monitor patients' response to treatment. Thanks to the flow of constantly updated real-time information produced by the gadgets, doctors and health workers can decide on quick choices about diagnoses and discover conditions that are getting worse or improving.

By giving patients tablets and RPM devices while they were asked to isolate at home, healthcare workers can reduce the influx of patients coming for check-up and admission. With regards to remote work, this has gone a long way to reducing the need to have medical experts to be available at all times and they can now attend to the needs of the patients remotely.

The pandemic has just quickened the existing innovative IoT solutions used in medical services. Truth be told, several medical experts are already making use of IoT for production processes. One case of IoT being utilized to decrease contact during the COVID-19 is when RPM innovation allows doctors to access patient information in real-time with the help of a secured cloud service.

In the delivery and logistics industry, organizations are using IoT gadgets to monitor resources as they are conveyed from one place to another, decreasing the requirement for physical examinations and information recording that requires employees to be present. These gadgets give constant information on a supply chain process involving location, temperature and if the product is tampered with, and integrity of the stock. With such relevant data, workers can settle on proactive choices to forestall potential issues and drive productivity, all from the comfort of their home.

With so much information now accessible at the team's disposal, and will continue to increase exponentially due to IoT innovations, organizations will then leverage on this information and transforming them into activities that help optimize the business. With the expansion of AI to IoT, businesses across sectors can make proactive, knowledgeable choices dependent on information gathered as a result of IoT, and eventually foresee future pattern and have solutions in place.

IoT Allows Remote Workers to Adjust to the "New Normal"

Just as IoT is a driving force for the transition into remote working, it is likewise providing the atmosphere for teams to adjust properly to this new reality as we look forward to the post-pandemic world. For instance, cities that are already tagged to be smart thanks to IoT can provide almost everything workers might need to effectively work from home.

IoT advances permit governments to track social distancing measures and trace contacts in an attempt to fight the spread of this infection, with smart cities turning out to be perfect examples of how IoT can help improve the safety of the general public. IoT-enabled gadgets are additionally giving an approach to diagnose possibilities of COVID-19 in a person with the help of connected thermometers that provide support to people trying to figure out if they have been exposed to the virus and when they might need to reach out for medical attention.

What's more, thanks to IoT smart gadgets in our homes help teams to communicate all the more serenely and effectively and thereby saving workers more time and cost. These innovative solutions include smart freezers that can take stocks of supplies and search for goods on the web. The Amazon Echo is a great example that permits users to control different gadgets from a center point, savvy temperature regulators and fittings that help people working from home optimize the use of energy, and smart bulbs that can be controlled from a central unit.

Security: Paramount for Safe IoT Usage

With the possibilities of an increase in the demand for IoT services, adequate security measures must be put in place to prevent hackers from taking advantage of our information and connectivity, while keeping workers safe as they work from home.

Those organizations that are just implementing IoT solutions due to the global pandemic and seeking to transition to the "new normal" workforce, they must have business-wide structures for procurement, implementation, security, and tracking of activities of IoT to help limit the possibilities of getting hacked. Likewise, IoT producers must guarantee that firmware goes through intensive security surveys and give low-level control of the equipment to ensure the safety of users.

Research has shown that a remarkable number of IoT-enabled innovative solutions are susceptible to getting hacked. Because of the possibilities of increasing cyber-attacks due to the disruption happening on a large scale, it's a higher priority than at any other time to ensure the safety of cloud systems and IoT gadgets.

Keeping up Business Continuity

Even with this global, most organizations have wound up performing incredibly. Carrying out business activities like before has been the transient objective of basically every business out there. Yet, to accomplish this, it is completely important to guarantee the safety of all workers involved.

While remote work is the most suggested choice today, getting a whole workforce off-premises, for the time being, has been incomprehensible for a ton of organizations. This is a cycle that requires significant investment, particularly when there is no experience on the issue. Here, IoT can be the path to consistent progress to the post-pandemic workforce.

Digitized Processes: This is the initial step to encouraging distant working. IoT innovations can uphold circuitous and direct tasks through cloud solutions. Thusly, teams can effectively take their work process from an on-location task to the cloud domain. In no time, an entire workforce will have the option to track the procedures of these IoT solutions and discuss plans over conference calls.

Limited Contact: When on-site workers are indispensable, physical distancing is a must. With the assent of workers and general public guidelines, an IoT system can be used to ensure basic safety measures at some critical point of operations of the business. While tracking activities with the help of IoT solutions will help organizations make well-informed decisions.

Management can be carried out remotely: In some areas where the government policies limit the possibilities of on-site work, IoT can be utilized to screen and control activities and equipment remotely. Allowing cloud-based IoT solutions to have basic control over some operations will permit workers to function effectively from home and maintain productivity with respect to all resources.

Creating Flexibility And Resilience

Going ahead, vulnerability is inescapable. We are yet to fully understand the difficulties that this new workforce will characterize. Indeed, even once the pandemic is over, we will be living in a new world. IoT innovative solutions can assist organizations with building the adaptability and strength they require to confront unexpected changes.

Comprehensive IT frameworks: Connectivity and Cybersecurity are the two focal points of IT solutions in businesses. In a worldwide distant work situation, they are a higher priority than at any other time. A cloud-based IoT system that connects workers with machines and gadgets is probably the most ideal approach to assemble solid safe connections to prevent hackers while keeping up productive work processes.

Cost Improvements: With the help of advanced analytic tools, IoT solutions can recognize key focuses for creating cost-effective upgrades for short term measures. This incorporates the viability, accessibility, quality, and execution of the workers and equipment as a whole. A system of sensors can likewise give continuous information on stock levels, production limit, and supply chain organization information.

Revenue can be predicted: Unexpected deeps are sure to happen. To keep deals and consumer loyalty up, organizations can utilize IoT to survey local and international market information and decide the best activities dependent on information gathered. IoT can even consider stock levels, scheduled production limits, and suggests periods that are best to produce and sell in the post-pandemic era.

Building A Long-Term Competitive Advantage

The post-COVID world will be powered by whatever business techniques we execute now. We are now observing the move to a contactless supply chain and personalized service delivery. In any case, the most important thing in this post-pandemic era is to come out of it as strong as conceivable from it. The best way to make this possible is to put certain IoT solutions in place that will help scale up the business over time.

Implementing Smart Takeover: Smart gadgets are the future of the home and work environment, and as I have mentioned earlier, the future is here. The pandemic has fast-track the future we were all expecting. The products and services that will prevail sooner rather than later are those that encourage personalization, communication, and easy to use.

Improving Supply Chain Processes: Availability of Data is perhaps the greatest test for the development of IoT solutions that are effective in supply chain processes. From organizing delivery schedules to overseeing stock quality, IoT is the ideal answer for reducing the need for the physical presence of employees and eventually cut down cost, reducing the risk present in the conventional supply chain processes, and uncovers information that boosts the supply process.

General Process Optimization: Powered by AI, an IoT system can deal with information from basically every business process or task procedure. When this is added to other IoT solutions like business management solutions, organizations can utilize IoT to rapidly plan for market changes.

IMPLEMENTING THE POWER OF IOT

Internet of things is having an incredible move of significance in the business world that will only get bigger with time. Since the IT sector is a significant sector of the general economy that has kept things the same, the capacity of IoT solutions remains the most reasonable alternative for business as we move forward.

It's been a couple of months since the pandemic started, things are beginning to settle. This is the opportunity to implement vital upgrades that will scale your businesses in the long run. The normal working models no longer work. It's an ideal opportunity to use innovation and actualize long term plans that will scale up your business.

CHAPTER FOUR

ARTIFICIAL INTELLIGENCE AND MACHINE LEARNING DEFINING THE FUTURE OF WORK.

As organizations implement innovative solutions that improve work processes and introduce artificial intelligence in business processes, the restricting element that continues to limit the transformation of these innovations into genuine business benefits will be the level of skilled workers involved. It is now evident that several task that were carried out by human workers in the past are no longer possible.

At the same time, the demand for these AI business solutions overwhelms supply at present, which shows that the fundamental barrier to implementing these AI solutions are not the availability of the innovation but the possibilities of organizations to have the right set of skilled workers to implement them successfully. We are in a different work order that requires, the right individuals with the correct abilities in the correct jobs to perform the correct task, and this will far exceed the importance of selecting the correct innovation to ensure normal business process in this era.

The ascent of AI and machine learning is additionally going to play a major role going forward.

One of the significant changes in the post-pandemic era is to see more organizations receiving a level working structure, where the roles of employees are less clear and the turnaround of fresh innovative skills is more noteworthy. In this new normal, a cutting edge working model that underpins the chance to learn skills, to have seasoned leaders give guidance, and to include digital remote workers to carry out important tasks will be important to help provide the best of products and services in this era.

By moving past a one-size-fits-all approach to deal with the workforce and management of business processes, AI solutions can help make the conditions wherein workers feel empowered by their work, valued by their organization, and glad to continue to work from home.

Tech-savvy organizations that are early adopters of AI workforce solutions have developed frameworks that allow workers learn while working via AI solutions, exploit new ways to do business, and at the same time reduce expenses, improve quality, create value and respond rapidly to the quick changing and rising transformations due to the global pandemic. But the main question now is how these solutions can be implemented across different businesses in different sectors of the economy.

The appropriate response may rely upon the capacity of corporate pioneers to re-settle the workforce and to re-consider hierarchical structures, by utilizing the same computerized advances that have destabilized it in any case. The approaching AI transformation ought to strengthen the exceptionally human qualities that characterize how we work, especially in the way that we team up and create connections with other employees and even customers. AI and machine learning are inevitable in this post-pandemic work force era.

AI AND MACHINE LEARNING GOING FORWARD

Alongside AI and ML, teams should be ready to improve their work with the help of digital workers like EaaS and RPA as discussed in subsequent chapters. When talking about enterprises, RPA, for instance, is about utilizing automated programming to carry out repetitive tasks, large scale processes that involve several steps and precision that would have previously required a human with high-end skills. Solutions like this will move the skilled workers to more required intelligent tasks. Rather than individuals going through hours finishing the same repetitive errands, they can use RPA to zero in on work that requires human inventiveness and imagination.

Interestingly, teams presently working from home are becoming acclimated to depending on AI solutions and embracing their new collaborative work environment. As they become more acquainted with these innovative solutions, they'll be more open to implementing measures that improve their productivity through machine learning.

The fear that AI will replace the workforce is no longer the main concern, the main concern now is to stay alive while we get work done. The issue to consider now is that AI will upgrade task and requirement of skilled workers requiring more insight and intellectual processes, which will be a major aspect of the post-pandemic workforce. As more states and nations request isolations and push for zero contact for getting basics things like medical and food supplies, there are limited options other than to get these jobs done with the help of AI and machine learning innovations.

It now obvious that AI and machine learning are not a treat to the conventional workforce but a tool to help make work easier, better, and productive. In a place where social distancing and isolation are the order of the day to help reduce the spread of the infection, AI, machine learning, digital workforce, and other innovative solution that will be discussed in the next chapter, will be necessary to get work done today and in the future. With AI and machine learning the workforce will never remain the same again, the new workforce era is here and it's an ideal opportunity to look into the future.

CHAPTER FIVE

TECHNOLOGY INNOVATION THAT WILL FOSTER THE FUTURE OF WORK

As the world is coming out of this global pandemic, technological innovations will be the spine to guarantee business coherence. Amid the pandemic, businesses will undoubtedly battle with limitation of resources, with their most noteworthy need is doing business as usual and keeping their current clients satisfied. In our present world of vulnerability — where our work environment, method of work, and even nature of work continues to change — innovation has an empowering tool that can assist us with adjusting rapidly and execute strategic needs to continue our work.

In one significant short-term surge, communication and advanced applications appear to have assumed control over the world. Teams from all over the globe are utilizing interpersonal organizations, joint effort instruments, internet learning stages, and web-based business applications to rebuild their work and life. Working remotely and virtual gatherings have become the new normal, and innovations that were maybe recognizable to just smaller tech networks are now becoming the main focus, taking the center stage of everything.

Combining technologies like rapid web, 4G/5G, data analytics, portable apps, cloud, man-made reasoning, AI, and mechanical technology are being tried and used to present creative methodologies. Consistent communication, joint effort, and innovations have gone from being just popular phases to becoming earnest necessities, reflecting on the important roles that innovation plays in reducing business focuses.

The ongoing spread of pandemic is rousing an ever-increasing number of organizations to request that staffs work from home. In any case, have they equipped their representatives to do as such? Current workplaces are equipped with innovation and foundation that makes work conceivable, yet most homes don't have a similar amount of that gadget to make work easier. If you're wanting to keep up efficiency levels at home, you'll have to augment the innovations that you currently utilizing. Falling behind on the team or in the organizations may truly affect your proficiency.

For those not used to working remotely, it probably won't be anything but easy to know where to start from. Here are some technological innovations that remote workers ought to consider to keep on with their work: As the world is coming out of this global pandemic, technological innovations will be the spine to guarantee business coherence. Amid the pandemic, businesses will undoubtedly battle with limitation of resources, with their most noteworthy need is doing business as usual and keeping their current clients satisfied. In our present world of vulnerability — where our work environment, method of work, and even nature of work continues to change — innovation has an empowering tool that can assist us with adjusting rapidly and execute strategic needs to continue our work.

In one significant short-term surge, communication and advanced applications appear to have assumed control over the world. Teams from all over the globe are utilizing interpersonal organizations, joint effort instruments, internet learning stages, and web-based business applications to rebuild their work and life. Working remotely and virtual gatherings have become the new normal, and innovations that were maybe recognizable to just smaller tech networks are now becoming the main focus, taking the center stage of everything.

Combining technologies like rapid web, 4G/5G, data analytics, portable apps, cloud, man-made reasoning, AI, and mechanical technology are being tried and used to present creative methodologies. Consistent communication, joint effort, and innovations have gone from being just popular phases to becoming earnest necessities, reflecting on the important roles that innovation plays in reducing business focuses.

The ongoing spread of pandemic is rousing an ever-increasing number of organizations to request that staffs work from home. In any case, have they equipped their representatives to do as such? Current workplaces are equipped with innovation and foundation that makes work conceivable, yet most homes don't have a similar amount of that gadget to make work easier. If you're wanting to keep up efficiency levels at home, you'll have to augment the innovations that you currently utilizing. Falling behind on the team or in the organizations may truly affect your proficiency.

For those not used to working remotely, it probably won't be anything but easy to know where to start from. Here are some technological innovations that remote workers ought to consider to keep on with their work:

ROBOTIC PROCESS AUTOMATION AND WHY IT'S NECESSARY.

Robotic Process Automation, also known as RPA, is a critical but often overlooked component of a digital enterprise. Many people think that digital enterprises involve writing a bunch of applications, which are then deployed by various means (cloud, mobile devices, etc.). RPA is a piece of highly customized software, often called a Software Robot or a BOT, sometimes Software-as-a-service that when deployed performs a variety of tasks as a part of the Digital Enterprise. BOTs facilitate inter-application messaging, manipulate data and output, or trigger responses.

RPA can also mimic human actions within an enterprise. Over the past years, RPA has become increasingly common as they are great at handling repeatable and predictive tasks. They have also shown to dramatically reduce costs, as well as increase effectiveness and agility, regardless of the use of on-premises or remote workforce.

Why We Need RPA For This New Workforce Era

More Accurate Work Done

RPA is more precise than manually accomplishing the work again and again. The software isn't inclined to human mistake and they don't get drained or distracted. There are no off-base subtleties going in an inappropriate field. The specific level of precision relies upon the optical character recognition (OCR) that the RPA programming uses. These frameworks catch enormous measures of information. In addition to what is to be processed, the framework records practically everything about the procedure it is asked to complete, including metadata about when it was done, how it was submitted, who inside the organization has seen it, and so forth.

No Down-Time

RPA software can work constantly – 24-hours per day each and every day of the year – at full capacity. RPA doesn't take a vacation, doesn't rest, won't need days off, and never has a "genuinely unproductive" day. It's entirely reasonable that human staff need those things. Bots help ensure there's the ideal opportunity for humans staff to make the most of their performances, get enough rest, and deal with their wellbeing instead of scrambling and staying at work longer than required to stay overtime to get the work done.

Expanded Productivity

The way that RPA can do nonstop handling and work without delay or need to fix mistakes implies it completes more work than a human staff could have done. Normally, an RPA can accomplish a task that will usually require about by 4 to 8 human workers. What's more, on the off chance that you had in-house staff who were taking care of such undertaking before you began utilizing RPA, they presently find the opportunity to concentrate their skill and strength on more profitable roles. In addition, having those tasks done consequently in an effective position makes it simpler for representatives to utilize the data, which builds their profitability also.

Quick Implementation

Setting up and running RPA goes rapidly. Actualizing another RPA programming framework surely happens a lot quicker than training a renewed individual. You can have RPA software fully operational in not more than a day. Interestingly, in the event that you needed to recruit another human staff you'd be setting aside some effort to figure out resumes, direct meetings, experience the employing procedure, and afterward, train them once you, at last, discover somebody.

Simple To Scale

If you ever get an excess of work for your RPA to deal with, there is a straightforward solution to that. Simply add extra RPA capacity. That is a lot simpler than recruiting and training new workers for the same task. RPA makes a framework that is exceptionally simple to scale with your developing business. You simply contact your RPA service supplier, let them realize what you need, and they'll get it set up in no time.

No Training Time

If thing change with the way you do business and your procedures change and the RPA need to find some new information, you can either supply them with new prompts or adjust their configurations. That goes a lot quicker than training workers for new tasks. What's more, that is likewise going to set aside some funds for you, because it would be expensive for an existing human worker to remove time from their main task and train for a new task or train new employees.

They'll Never Quit

With RPA, you don't need to stress over workers stopping or managing turnover. RPA couldn't care less how hard they're functioning, regardless of whether they're upbeat in their occupations, or what number of redundant undertakings they stick out with. They never resign or see a new opportunity to move onward to an alternate job. To put it plainly, RPA means you'll never need to stress over recruiting and preparing new staff for the same task again.

Repatriate Jobs

Individuals are frequently worried about RPA removing employments from real individuals. Be that as it may, most of the activities carried out by RPA are mostly outsourced to overseas workers through EaaS and outsourcing, so many organizations aren't recruiting local workers for those assignments. They're outsourcing such takes abroad. Since the RPA would be overseen/facilitated by a reputable firm, utilizing RPA really repatriates employments.

More tight Security

At the point when human representatives are doing some sensitive task, there's consistently a specific measure of risk involved. Nobody likes to find out that staff is double-crossing them, yet these things do happen within organizations. Also, if you don't trust your employee, having them enter sensitive information can at present be a security concern. RPA doesn't want to know the significance of the information they are working with, which ensures the safety of your merchants and customers. Additionally, RPA doesn't need to spare/retain passwords like a human so there's less danger of secret word penetrate.

Insignificant IT Resources

Keeping up programming bots requires a negligible IT experience. Most times, IT doesn't have to get involved in the implementation process. Your RPA frameworks will be overseen by the product supplier. They are liable for support, updates, and so on. That takes the weight off IT (which most likely as of now has more work than they can deal with) and saves you more revenue from that end.

Implementing RPA To Build The New Workforce

RPA can be implemented in any type of organization. There are various use cases extending from IT framework to marketing to procurement and so on. Organization cuts across all sectors and ventures. When you choose you need to utilize RPA for the information section, you simply need to discover a product supplier to work with. Get one that is good with your ERP framework and they'll deal with practically everything else.

CLOUD COMPUTING

It is anything but difficult, to sum up, that innovation has helped organizations to continue working during the coronavirus episode. In any case, digging further into what precisely has been the way to empowering individuals to telecommute and keep business-basic administrations going, there is one steady, cloud computing.

While any semblance of Zoom and Microsoft Teams are picking up a foothold with users and organizations the same, the explanation a huge number of individuals can utilize this tech all the while is a direct result of the advantages of cloud computing.

These advantages are very much diverse and cloud system empowers organizations to scale here and there with adaptability so they can adapt to unpredictable conditions like those at present being experienced, while Software-as-a-service (SaaS), Employee-as-a-service (EaaS), mean organizations don't need to stress over scaling up their equipment and data transfer capacity to adapt to immense requests.

Cloud innovation empowers staff to remain at home. Contingent upon the kind of business, the advantages of cloud computing may change. For example, for some companies, it will essentially be the situation of encouraging the new normal 'remote working.'

At no other point in time has there ever been such a requirement for the moment accessibility of IT assets empowered by the cloud than during this coronavirus pandemic. The cloud keeps on changing networks among individuals and organizations on a worldwide scale. The cloud is all over the place; in our vehicles, on our TV screens, in our telephones, and even in our watches.

Without the cloud, we will be unable to do a large number of the things we do each day—a rundown that has developed exponentially during this global pandemic. For instance, it would be all the more trying for the management of organizations to get to business data for their organizations from anyplace on the planet. Organizations would likewise make some harder memories sharing and managing reports effectively, with workers that are thousands of miles away – and even in their city. Indeed, even short physical distance would create a problem for a coordinated effort between employees without the cloud.

There are a few different business-basic everyday exercises and functionalities empowered by the cloud that would be lost, or eased back down if not for present-day cloud innovations, including:

The Cloud Enables Remote Work.

Even though numerous entrepreneurs and CEOs never figured they would need to have their entire workforce working remotely, here we are. What's more, the expense of losing months, weeks, or even only one day, of efficiency is startling, if not deadly. Empowering staff to work at a similar limit as they do nearby is priceless at a time this way. Uncertain of what the future will hold, the far off limit of the cloud appears to be more urgent than any other time in recent memory.

With the assistance of cloud server firms, organizations can bolster WFH exercises. Work and joint effort can proceed as normal thanks to memory, stockpiling, and handling power that reacts to request and assured access to information.

At that point, utilizing virtual work areas, teams can sign in from any gadget – and from anyplace – and get back on track. With the capacity to utilize similar applications and projects they are familiar with, there's consistent progress to working in the workplace, at home, or in a hurry. Additionally, all the figuring power is conveyed by the cloud, so even low-limit PCs can deal with overwhelming outstanding tasks at hand. This purposes a large number of the security and limit issues gave bring-your-own-gadget arrangements.

The Cloud Ensures Availability.

Cloud systems are intended for flexible appropriation and high accessibility. In any event, when you have such a significant number of individuals communicating and getting to information contemporary, cloud suppliers can keep up. They exploit numerous server networks and move remaining tasks at hand to convey continuous assistance. VPNs, then again, frequently aren't prepared to scale to that level and give indications of stress when utilization surpasses the ordinary limit.

The Cloud Helps Cut the Upkeep.

Cloud conditions take out inner IT support tasks and permit organizations to pull together staff time and vitality to more important endeavors. Under normal conditions, this saves more money and big benefits.

In the current pandemic circumstance, this is a tremendous bit of leeway. On-premises and conventional server farms are kept up by IT specialists, important faculty who will be unable to work distantly. Be that as it may, who can keep these physical frameworks working if even experts are on lockdown? Rather, the cloud specialist organization and the IT staff can react to demands essentially. This is another reason why more organizations in recent times are thinking about cloud structures.

Fast Data

From AI to big data, fast information processing frameworks, for things like, research, data analysis, and assembling. Cloud systems put things together, make systems uniform, and carry out these responsibilities flawlessly with the goal that solutions can rapidly develop for issues and difficulties that come up. In this day and age, going to and fro to the supercomputer isn't a need any longer when the cloud itself is the gigantic supercomputer.

A Time for Action

Current companies have consistently relied on an advanced framework to help their organizations. With the beginning of limitations, COVID-19 has made, more organizations are perceiving the certain worth that cloud conveys. Maybe the most phenomenal thing about cloud advances is the adaptable alternatives they give; significantly more so now in this season of emergency, when organizations need arrangements they can execute and test rapidly. A huge, ceaseless system of cloud-based frameworks empowered our general surroundings to keep awake and running all through this pandemic, with not very many issues.

Exactly what number of more different thoughts and organizations will begin with the assistance of the cloud due to the coronavirus emergency and characterize how we communicate with innovation in the post-COVID-19 time? I am certain that as a general public, we will advance out of this emergency, and the cloud will keep on being a principal empowering agent for a considerable length of time to come.

I additionally envision a flood of noxious assaults searching for weaknesses on cloud foundations set up hurriedly during and the COVID-19 pandemic. That is the reason it is important that the information security act is actualized appropriately by an expert. At the point when it's set accurately, the cloud has adaptable security controls that give an elevated level of protection against disavowal of-administration assaults and other digital dangers.

Given that, this is not the time to keep thinking of how to move to the cloud. It's an ideal opportunity to make the move. Since virtual and remote working is probably going to stay long after the pandemic is no more.

Microsoft Dynamics business applications platform. A cloud-based encompassing solution that brings a range of CRM and ERP applications, it's as of now being proclaimed as the future of business software and indicates to have large advantages for organizations. So what's the serious deal?

Microsoft as of now has a large share of the business programming market, with its set-up of Dynamics applications have been around for a long time. With Microsoft Dynamics, the organization is moved all the requirements of a business into one package, while liberating businesses from the weight of a physical framework by working through the cloud framework. It comes with a lot of benefits that come in handy for business management activities in this post-pandemic era and the new normal of working from home. Some of these benefits include:

Expanded adaptability (and diminished expenses)

This solution provides a tailored model that clients don't have to burden themselves with a solid set-up of applications they don't need. Rather, organizations can choose the applications they need, and create a custom-made package that best accommodates their needs.

Microsoft dynamic additionally has its own application store that comes with other Microsoft- add-ins and extensions to assist you to streamline your solution to your own, business requirements.

Its cloud-based nature additionally gives adaptability of access as well. With its online interface, all clients need is a web connection so as to interface with and work with Dynamics 365, which means your team can complete things whenever anyplace.

Smart, business insights

Bringing all your business needs into one package is the best solution to improve productivity, and can assist you with becoming familiar with your business ideas. This solution makes use of Microsoft's AI-mixed business insight device Power BI, to insightful reports through intelligent data analysis bringing revealing and logical capacity to your business information.

Power BI's dashboards are locally incorporated with the Dynamics 365 applications, so you can get all the insight you need from inside one interface. Breaking down information from over your whole steady of Microsoft items, Power BI can give firm, noteworthy input, make forecasts about new chances, and visualize your information in manners that drive insightful decisions.

Improved efficiency

Separating information storehouses and permitting business applications to share data creates a connected framework, giving your team access to all the information they need in one spot. Having a total image of your company and its work processes will assist users with working all the more productively. Having one comprehensive information storage as an establishment for your applications likewise nullifies the requirement for time-sucking copy information passage.

With inbuilt automated capacities, like in cases of RPA, Dynamics can assist with some of your simple tasks, while pointing you the correct way on huge tasks.

Improved security and consistence

With all the item foundation based off-site, staying up with the latest, practical, and secure no longer tumbles to you and your IT office. Microsoft handles the entirety of the back-end systems at their end, so you can rest adequately without stressing that you passed up a great opportunity one of the workplace PCs when introducing the most recent security fix.

The stage's security model likewise guarantees the respectability and protection of your information. Right off the bat, you'll never lose your information, as it is securely upheld up in Microsoft's protected cloud. Besides, you have full authority over the information that clients approach, which means your clients are never gathering to any data they don't have to know to carry out their responsibilities. With Microsoft server farms presently situated the world over, your information won't just be secure, yet completely consistent with nearby laws.

A less complex, comprehensive method of working

Elements 365 offers a bound together, easy to use interface which gives your group all that they have to carry out their responsibility; no additionally fluttering between applications, or moving information across programs. Its recognizable, Microsoft-dynamic interface can likewise help support client selection with regards to revealing your new arrangement.

A shelter for Citizen Developers everywhere throughout the world, Dynamics 365 likewise makes it simpler for clients to redo their answer and make new applications with programs like Microsoft Flow. A cloud-based program that encourages clients to rapidly incorporate different arrangements into your Dynamics applications, Microsoft Flow can even assist you with making work processes dependent on those outside connections. Let's assume you need to execute a social listening technique as a major aspect of your promoting plan; by coordinating Twitter with Dynamics 365, you can set up a work process to make another lead in your Sales application each time somebody tweets a specific word or expression.

Additionally remembered for the 365 bundles is Power Apps, another device that empowers clients to manufacture portable applications that meet their individual needs. The intuitive idea of the application manufacturer implies clients can fabricate applications without the requirement for complex code, engaging clients to modify their answer and guarantee they capitalize on its usefulness.

Obviously, Microsoft is overly enthusiastic about the entirety of their items playing pleasantly together, and Dynamics 365 is the encapsulation of hyper-associated programming. Elements 365 not just has a comparative look to other Microsoft programming, it additionally joins their highlights, which means you can make archives and track messages from inside its interface.

With the entirety of your applications ready to converse with one another and share data, Dynamics 365 can do supportive easily overlooked details like show past contact and relationship data when you get an email, or remind you to include an arrangement in your schedule if a client requests to be reached on a particular date. Elements 365 likewise flaunt local highlights which recently required outsider additional items, for example, the following email opens and snaps through.

With Dynamics, so a solution that is very important in this pandemic era, it'll be sometime before we see to what extent it can deliver on such big promises. In the meantime, let's consider other business solutions.

Adaptive WiFi

While a vehicle, bicycle, or open transportation may regularly help manage your movements, Wi-Fi permits you to productively and dependably drive to your advanced work environment. To remain associated with your colleagues, you need web access that reacts to your requirements progressively. Enter Adaptive WiFi.

Not at all like the work the conventional Wi-Fi, Adaptive Wi-Fi makes use of AI to outline where and when your home and gadgets use Wi-Fi the most. It at that point allots the proper data transfer capacity as required. Consider it your traffic-regulator for all the gadgets connected in your home. This framework ensures that not exclusively does everything in your home get the Wi-Fi it needs, yet in addition that mostly utilized gadgets get the most remarkable and secure service. Adaptable Wi-Fi supplier Plume offers items that progressively answers to your necessities, yet additionally, give online security to assurance on-line safety during utilization.

Virtual Meetings

This fast transformation to remote work over should be classified as the Zoom era, one of the world's most mainstream conference platform has made record increases in usage as workers work from home.

Up close and personal meetings are the foundation of numerous organizations; taking that factor out completely is not possible. Apps like Zoom, Skype, and Google Hangouts make it simple to keep in contact with associates or customers across distance. While video calls probably won't have a similar vibe as in-person gatherings, they give a successful substitute on occasions such as these.

Instant Communication Tools

As supportive as video visits maybe, not all situations need up close and personal solutions. When working remotely, you'll have to literarily speak with your team. While email might be the go-to, continually invigorating your inbox and arranging your messages can be time draining. Twenty-eight percent of the normal workday is spent on email alone. Instant talk service providers like Slack, Telegram, and Quip let you experience the simplicity of in-office correspondence over the web. With the capacity to discuss personal or as a team, you can guarantee that whoever needs to see your message will do so momentarily.

Business Management Platforms

Most organizations utilize an undertaking in the management stage. These, however, take on new degrees of significance as workers begin to work from home. Without the capacity to check in normally face to face, keeping in touch with various plans and items can immediately get the business in a bad position. While these issues aren't easily solved, merging your organization resources in one management platform like Microsoft Dynamics is a decent spot to begin.

Regardless of whether you use Asana, Trello, or something different altogether, ensure all that you're dealing with is unmistakably divided on your desired platform. Business management software recommends setting out a task the board plan for your work at an opportune time; it's critical for guaranteeing that things don't veer off course later down the line. Consistently give reports on how your tasks are going along, and urge your teammates to do likewise — this can help cut down on pointless meetings.

Digital Assistants

The need for digital assistant solutions has increased consistently over the years, so there's a decent possibility there's as of now one in your home. Regardless of whether it's an Amazon Echo, a Google Assistant, or a Siri-empowered Apple item, most specialists are now to some degree acquainted with digital assistants. Be that as it may, few areas of now utilizing them to their maximum ability to work remotely.

Digital assistants can make calls, send messages, take notes, and accomplish such a great deal more. While utilizing one in the workplace may ordinarily be disruptive, utilizing one at home can help you to keep on filling in as you cook, clean, or perform other significant family obligations. Some digital assistants can likewise help you hold conference calls without the troublesome coordination they normally require.

As remote working turns into an essential reality for an ever-increasing number of people, some may battle to adjust to the new condition. While the change can be a long way from simply using innovation for your potential benefit can make settling in much better.

Supportive Technologies

Savvy organizations manage digital gadgets provided to workers to make working from home better with:

VPN: A virtual private system is the most basic innovation of all. It gives a safe correspondence channel through open Internet associations.

VoIP: Voice over Internet Protocol cuts correspondence expenses and expands team adaptability. With VoIP, team members can connect to their office calls from anyplace, send texts, forward calls to cell phones, video chat with customers and collaborators, and the sky is the limit from there.

Information Backup/Recovery: Keeping basic information safe is always an issue. So ensure staffs working form home have backup solutions provided to them. They ought to have an auxiliary backup framework also. Survey strategies with them to ensure they're backing up.

System Security: Network security is a principal. Getting hacked can cost you large dollars and make a lot of terrible mistakes. Hackers can likewise block effectiveness and profitability.

Malware Protection: Another must-have. Most PCs come standard with firewall and antivirus insurance. Move up to business-proficient security arrangements. What's more, keep steady over updates.

Interactive Tech Tools: These are the way to expanding team productivity and proficiency. Think applications like SharePoint, Microsoft Linc, and GoTo Meeting. Working from home can be impossible without these.

Combine all of these innovations, great IT support, and technical service providers. Together, this will save your cash, time, and disappointment. Building a remote workforce can bring the ultimate break through you need to get by in the present global pandemic era. The key is consolidating the correct innovations with the ideal individuals. Together, they'll make a far off workforce that reduces expenses, expands efficiency, and produces brand-building client encounters.

CONCLUSION

Society all in all has experienced radical changes because of the COVID-19 pandemic. Among the most noteworthy was the transformation from in-office to remote work across different ventures everywhere throughout the world. The unexpected surge in work-from-home developed the reason for a global conversation with respect to best practices for connecting the workforce from different locations. And with the look of things, we might not have been adequately prepared for this but we are coming out stronger and united.

I will leave you with this optimistic note. In the course of my life, I have seen we humans make the best of our lives through innovations and digital transformation with prominent steps in improving the human condition in the entirety of our archived history. Innovations have lifted more individuals out of extreme poverty, and with the advent of great innovations like the Internet, AI, and so on, we have connected most parts of the world together. It is with this view I remain optimistic and appreciative of the universal connectivity we are enjoying right now.

Indeed, even organizations that were impervious to the idea of a digital workforce have been compelled to permit workers to work from home, for tasks to be carried out while avoiding potential risk to stop the spread of the infection. While the capacity to work from home is an advantage that numerous workers love, so many organizations come up short on the innovative structure to offer that ability without certain losses due to the inability to continue the conventional way of work. However, one thing to look out for with the global pandemic is that organizations understand the advantages of optimizing digital transformation.

While a few organizations will inevitably return to the usual work-in-office arrangements, it's normal that some will understand the advantages to the new normal way to get work done and it can very well be done to increase the productivity of the organization. If nothing else, they will have important experience about what is required and how to oblige telecommute needs later on when it's required if there is a reason for everyone to return back home in the future.

The future is here!

You can reach out to Amit via LinkedIn https://www.linkedin.com/in/amit-loyd-augustine/?trk=author_mini-profile_title

About The Author

Amit Loyd Augustine is a technology advisor, consultant, and coach that advocates for enabling business growth through digital transformation. With over a decade of work experience in several top innovative business services. Having worked with Leading IT company as a Tech Support Associate, moving up the ranks to become a manager in no time and then becoming a Business Development Manager, Amit have had to collaborate with teams from across the globe creating an intelligent business solution for top brands and pioneering webinars and seminars that promote the integration of innovative solutions into business practices.

Amit Loyd Augustine has been an advocate of collaborative workforces, remote working, and employee satisfaction, long before the global pandemic. He is passionate about solving complex business technology problems by using simple techniques. For a more specific solution on how to take your business to the next level with digital transformative initiative. Amit can be of great help. He can also assist you in assessing the Total cost of Ownership on both models, absolutely free!

You can reach out to Amit via LinkedIn https://www.linkedin.com/in/amit-loyd-augustine/

About The Book

Post Pandemic Workforce Transformation ~ The Future of Work in the Post Pandemic Era by Amit Loyd Augustine is a book that discusses how business can transform from the in-office style of work to the new normal, which is the work-from-anywhere style. In this book, Amit provides great insight into what to expect in the post-pandemic era and the suggestion of innovative tools that can help make this process seamless. The Post Pandemic Workforce Transformation book is an enlightening masterpiece that any business or person looking to improve productivity while implementing measures to get work done with resources from anywhere in the world.